MORE Brief Prayers for Bread and Cup

For Elders at the Communion Table

D1598839

MORE
Brief Prayers
for
Bread and Cup

by Russell F. Harrison

CBP Press
St. Louis, Missouri

Address: CBP Press
          Box 179
          St. Louis, MO 63166

Library of Congress Cataloging-in-Publication Data

Harrison, Russell F., 1918-
    More brief prayers for Bread and Cup.

    Continues: Brief prayers for Bread and Cup.
                ©1976
    1. Lord's Supper—Prayer-books and devotions—
    English.
I. Title.
BV826.5.H37   1986   264'.36   86-6076
ISBN 0-8272-2319-6

Printed in the United States of America

Introduction

Communion is central to the life of the church. The role of the elders is a key to the richness intended.

I am humbled by your response to my first book for elders titled *Brief Prayers for Bread and Cup*. I hope that the emphasis on *brevity* in communion prayers contributed to the fine reception of my effort.

Now, I present *More Brief Prayers for Bread and Cup*. May these brief prayers stimulate and encourage you to think about and plan carefully *your* prayers at the table. Remember that you are leading others in moments of prayer and meditation.

There is a useful pattern in preparing or writing a communion prayer. These four elements can be your continuing guide:

1. *Thanksgiving* (to God)
2. *Remembrance* (of Jesus)
3. *Presence* (of the Holy Spirit)
4. *Dedication* (to serve)

You will see these reflected to a greater or lesser degree in each of the prayers of this book. Variety of emphasis may be necessary. Because of the *brevity* of these prayers, only one of these four elements may be stressed.

The communion elements are not only biblical but are part of the rich tradition of the church. May your prayers at the Lord's Table be an inspiration and provide encouragement to your own congregation. Be brief. The Spirit of God will do the rest.

Russell F. Harrison

An Elder's Prayer of Commitment

Almighty God, thank you for the privilege of being an elder.

I am not worthy of this great responsibility.

Guide my thoughts in preparation of a prayer for bread and cup.

Help me to remember that my prayer is but one of many prayers in the worship service so that my focus may be sharp and clear. Make it truly a *communion* prayer.

Most gracious God, grant that my voice may reflect reverence and confidence so that others may be led to a deeper searching of their own lives in prayer.

May I remember, O God, to speak clearly and distinctly so that no one may lose the meaning of my prayer offered for the bread or cup.

Keep me mindful of the purpose and place of my communion prayer among other prayers in the service of worship.

Enable me, O God, to lead others in thanksgiving, in remembrance of Jesus, in experiencing the presence of your Holy Spirit, and in dedicating their lives for Christian witness and service. Amen.

We are grateful, O God, for the dawning of each new day and for food that sustains our physical being. We come to the Lord's Table giving thanks for this spiritual bread. We remember Jesus, taking bread, breaking it, and saying, "This is my body, broken for you." Now, O God, we pray for a renewed awareness of your presence as we commit our lives to serving in more effective ways in the days that you may grant to us. Amen.

O God, who created us in your image and who blesses our lives so richly from day to day, we give thanks for this cup of salvation. We recall the suffering of Jesus and his death upon the cross so that we might have eternal life. Guide us by your Holy Spirit into newness of life. Alone, most loving God, we cannot find fullness and completeness. With the strength you can give us, we find hope. As we drink the cup, may we rededicate all that we have and are. Amen.

9

Eternal God, we are thankful for your abiding presence. We remember the love that surrounds us as we partake of the bread in memory of Jesus. May your Holy Spirit be within and among us. Help us, O God, to be instruments of your love as we eat the bread from this communion table and dedicate ourselves more fully to serving you and others during this coming week. Amen.

 Blessed God, with prayers of thanksgiving we receive this cup, seeking to renew our minds and hearts. We remember Jesus, whose sacrificial love has brought us together here this day. Grant us a fuller sense of your presence as we come around the Lord's Table. Be with us, God, guiding us in daily living so that we may become worthy of all you have done for us. Deepen our dedication and commitment, we pray. Amen.

Almighty God, we give thanks for daily bread and for this bread of the Spirit that we share together in these moments of communion. We remember Jesus, our Savior who died on the cross, and we ask that your Spirit may guide us as we pray. Help us, O God, in the rededication of our lives to your service and our witness in daily living throughout the coming week. Amen.

Most merciful God, in thanksgiving we take the cup, remembering Jesus in the upper room with his disciples. We call upon you, O God, to be present among us with the gift of your Spirit. May your Holy Presence be a strength to us in hours of need. In the drinking of the cup, we commit ourselves to more effective Christian service. In prayerful quiet, we bring all that we have and are, asking you to use us in Christ's name. Amen.

11

O God of all time, you have been our help in ages past, our hope for years to come. Be thou our guide while life shall last, and our eternal home. We give thanks for daily bread and for the communion bread, which represents to us the broken body of Christ. We break the bread in his name and ask your presence now as we bring our personal prayers to you. As we begin a new week, we ask your continued guidance. In renewed dedication we seek to do your will. Amen.

 Most loving God, we express in thanksgiving our gratitude that we are privileged to come to this table on the Lord's Day. As we give thanks for the fruit of the vine, may we have a new sense of Jesus and his meaning in our lives. May this cup be a cup of blessing, O God. Fill us with the light of your presence. With deepened commitment, may we face each new day of this coming week assured that we are not alone. Amen.

Eternal Spirit, empower us as we come around this table to give thanks for daily bread, and as we break the bread that represents to us the broken body of Jesus. As we remember him, make your presence felt more keenly so that our moments of rededication may reflect your will for our daily living. Amen.

God of life and keeper of our souls, we acknowledge our dependence upon your sustaining love. In reverence we take this cup, which reminds us once again of Jesus and his blood that was shed for us. May your presence enliven our spirits and quicken our conscience so that our prayers of commitment may result in true service to you and to those about us in the days ahead. Amen.

Most gracious God, may the joy of being Christian be evident in our lives. Let the breaking of bread be for us a time of celebration because Jesus has come and because he bids us to follow him. Grant to us a happy and outgoing faith, so others cannot help knowing that we are Christians by our love. Be present with us now so that we may be refreshed, renewed, and enabled to witness more effectively for you. Amen.

 Infinite God, whose timeless presence has guided your children throughout the many centuries and continues as our guiding light today, we thank you for this cup of blessing. Enhance our desire to become better and more worthy Christians. We seek your promised presence as we eat this bread and drink this cup, remembering Jesus, who gave his all for each one of us. Make us more grateful for the everyday blessings, and use us, O God. Amen.

14

O loving and forgiving God, we bring into your presence our hopes, dreams, problems, anxieties, joys, and sorrows, because you are our God. We give thanks for the bread that is broken and given to each one of us during this memorable act of communion in the name of Jesus. Fill us with the power of your Holy Spirit as we serve during this coming week. Amen.

Everlasting yet ever-present God, we come to this communion table and receive the cup of salvation and blessing. In memory of Jesus and in gratitude for what he has meant to our lives, we give thanks. Help us to grow in our mission of witness and service to all people. Empower our rededication and commitment to living each day for you and for your world. Amen.

God of tender mercies, thank you for our daily bread and now for this bread of the spirit that we break together. Fill each one here with a sense of your abiding and guiding presence. Be with us in these moments of renewal as we prepare for the task of being living servants. We seek to fulfill your will now and day-to-day during this coming week. Amen.

 Compassionate God, look with favor upon our effort to learn and follow in your way. As we receive the cup, may it be in a moment of self-examination and prayer. Help us, O God, to understand Jesus better as we remember his life, his selfless ministry, and his death upon the cross for the sake of each one of us and for all humanity. Use us in the days ahead. Amen.

O God, we come to this table, a central element of our worship this Sunday morning, with praise and thanksgiving. We are grateful for the gift of life. As we see the beginning of another week, we break bread, asking that in this act of worship its significance may become more meaningful in each of our lives. Bless each unspoken prayer that in silence we place before you, O God. Amen.

May this cup be a cup of blessing to each one present, as it reminds us once again of your unfailing love. We give thanks for Jesus and his sacrifice that we might be redeemed. May our hearts and minds, O God, be open to the leading of your Holy Spirit. In confidence and assurance, we call upon you to use us according to your will as we seek to bear witness to the truth. Amen.

Most patient God, in humility we come before you with gratitude for our many blessings, especially for daily bread. Now we come to this communion time to remember Jesus, our Lord and our Savior. As we bring our individual prayers of commitment, fill us, O God, with the reality of your presence in our lives. You know our needs. Use us in your service in the week that lies ahead. Amen.

 Our Creator and our God, we give thanks for the beauty, wonder, and mystery of all you have created to enhance our lives. We take the cup and drink together as we reflect on the upper room and what Jesus commissioned us to do in remembrance of him. Enlighten our lives, O God, with the light of your presence, during these moments of prayerful communion. We rededicate ourselves this day to more effective Christian service. Amen.

Our everlasting God, we pause to praise
you and give thanks for the bread of life,
which we receive here at the table of
communion. Our thoughts turn to Jesus
as we remember his sacrifice on the
cross for all people everywhere and for
all time. May your presence, O God, be
made real to us in the breaking of bread.
Hear our prayers for renewal of our
lives. Bless our daily efforts to serve during this coming week. Amen.

Forgiving God, we know that we have
fallen short of your will for us many
times. We are grateful that in the receiving of this cup we find assurance of your
forgiveness. Cause us to recall Jesus and
the institution of this Lord's Supper in
that upper room with his disciples. We
pray, O God, for the power and presence
of your Holy Spirit as we partake together.
In dedication we offer our individual
prayers that you may strengthen our
daily living. Amen.

Generous God, whose gift of daily bread nourishes our physical bodies, we come to be enriched as we break the bread. We recall to our minds the sacrifice of Jesus for us. We remember him and also acknowledge his continued presence. We call upon you to fill us with the Holy Spirit as we rededicate our lives to your service. Amen.

 O God, help us to realize more fully that life is at its best when lived for others. As we give thanks for this cup, impress upon our minds and hearts our need for your Spirit within us. We come to this table not because we must but in answer to the invitation of Jesus. We need your continuing presence and guidance in daily living. Amen.

Caring God, whose blessings we cannot count, we give thanks for daily bread so needed by our physical being. Thank you for making provision to nourish our spiritual being through the breaking of this communion bread and eating it in the name of Jesus. Fill us with your Spirit, O God, so that our judgments may be wise and our service may be acceptable in your sight. Amen.

Almighty God, ruler of the universe and giver of the breath of life to each one of us, we give thanks for this cup. We remember Jesus and his willingness to give his life for us. With the promise of eternal life, we ask your Spirit to guide and direct us. With renewed commitment, we leave this table to live in such a way that we may be more pleasing to you as our God. Amen.

21

O God of love and compassion, thank you for the physical bread necessary for the continuation of our lives. May we sense as clearly our need for the spiritual bread provided at this communion table. Be present within us in our prayers of commitment so that our daily lives may reflect your will fulfilled each day. Amen.

 Bless this cup, O God, reminding us of Jesus, who endured suffering on the cross because of the victory over death that was to come. May your presence now so enrich our spirits that this coming week will find us more willing and able to be your servants in this world. Use us, O God, in your mission this coming week. Amen.

O God, who knows our every weakness yet empowers us with strength to serve, we thank you for our daily bread, as did Jesus when he taught his disciples to pray. In breaking bread together at his table, we seek the spiritual strength so necessary if we are to serve in your Kingdom. Fill our lives with your Spirit so that we may be able to fulfill our commitment. Amen.

Ever-present God, be near to those who turn to you in thanksgiving, praise, and prayer. Bless the cup as we partake of it in memory of Jesus. We acknowledge his continuing presence in the lives of those who seek his salvation. Be present within us, O God, so that these moments of renewal will bring us to active witness for you in the days that lie ahead. Use us daily in your service. Amen.

With thanksgiving, we share together in the eating of this bread. It reminds us once again that Jesus gave his life so that we might be redeemed. For the love and sacrifice he made, we are truly grateful. May we sense your presence as we worship in this time of communion. Empower us, O God, to a fuller commitment to your service. Amen.

 With thankful hearts we receive the cup, and in prayerful dedication we search our lives, O God. Our thoughts are of the upper room where this service began. We think of Jesus, who assured us of his presence at the Lord's Table through the centuries. May your Spirit be with us here this day, O God. With your guidance we can renew our dedication to Christian living in the days that lie ahead. Amen.

God of eternal love, as the daily bread sustains our physical bodies, may the breaking of communion bread sustain our spirits. For this we give thanks. In memory of Jesus and what he has done to save us, we ask your divine presence. We renew our commitment, and we will seek to live more Christian lives this coming week. Amen.

We are grateful for your abiding presence, God, as we take this cup in covenant together at this, the Lord's Table. It reminds us once again of your abiding love made manifest in the sending of your Son. O God, may your Holy Spirit open our eyes to the opportunities given us daily to witness to the good news of Jesus Christ. Amen.

Grant us, O God, the spirit, heart, and mind to be grateful, as we come in prayer to this communion table. Thank you for the food of this week and for this opportunity to partake of the spiritual bread in the name of Jesus. May we sense your presence, O God, in the breaking of bread and in our prayers of renewal and dedication. Guide us through the coming week. Amen.

 For the privilege of receiving this cup of blessing today, we give our thanks, O Lord. We come asking forgiveness for our many shortcomings and our sins. Help us to remember that Jesus died so that we might be forgiven and redeemed. Be present in our midst so that we might be guided by your Holy Spirit. Instill within us a new determination to live more fully the Christian way. Amen.

Merciful God, even when we are not deserving, we receive more of your blessings than we can count. We thank you for our daily bread. We bow in prayer and thanksgiving as we break the bread in this communion hour. Help us to remember Jesus and his meaning for our lives. Bless each prayer of rededication in the silence of these moments. Guide us this week, O God. Amen.

Gracious God, make us more appreciative of the beauty you have created to surround us. In drinking of the cup, may we see the beauty of our life, redeemed and bought with so great a price. May your Spirit be within us as we recall that upper room and what is required of us as followers of Christ. In commitment, may we go forth from this place to serve you in the days ahead. Amen.

Forgive us, O God, where we have failed you and one another. Accept our thanks for each day's bread and especially, on this Sunday morning, for the bread of the Lord's Table. In memory of Jesus and in dedication to living more useful lives, we invoke your blessing. We ask you to be present with us in the week to come. Amen.

 Creator of all people everywhere and in all time, we marvel at the mysteries of your creative power in human life. May this cup, in memory of Jesus, inspire us to better living in the days that lie ahead. Fill us with your Spirit so that we might become improved servants, seeking in company with millions everywhere to build your Kingdom here on earth. Amen.

Eternal God, who hears and answers prayer, we come to this table in thanksgiving for unrequested daily blessings that give us life itself. As physical food nourishes our bodies, may this communion bread remind us of the broken body of Christ, who died on the cross so that we might be saved. May your Spirit surround us as we rededicate all that we have and are to serving you. Amen.

As we take the cup, cleanse us of all unworthiness, so that we may be receptive to the presence of your Holy Spirit. We remember Jesus, on the night when he was betrayed, gathering with his disciples in the upper room. How grateful we are for his sacrificial love! Be with us now as we pray for strength to be renewed. May we seek to serve wherever we may be from day to day throughout the coming week. Amen.

O God, the giver of our daily bread, we pause to give you thanks. As we break the bread together, we ask that your presence might be felt here among us. In memory of Jesus we partake of his body, broken for us. Use us as your instruments of reconciliation and service throughout the days ahead. Amen.

 O God of grace, bless this cup, which helps us to remember Jesus and the manner in which his life was given for each one of us. May your Spirit empower us to overcome our blindness and our weakness so that we might be of greater service to your Kingdom. In humility, and yet in confidence, we pray for your continuing guidance. Amen.

Make us mindful, O Lord, of our debt to you for giving us daily bread for many days, weeks, and years. Renew us as we break together the communion bread of the Spirit. In the quiet of these moments, grant us a sense of renewed faith. We pledge ourselves to greater service in the coming days. Amen.

God of time and eternity, we are grate- ful for this communion hour. May partaking of the cup prepare us spiritually for the task of being Christian in our daily relationships. Help us, O God, to see more clearly your mission for us in the world today. With your help we can bring a better world into being. Amen.

Sustaining God, who loves and cares for us, we praise you. We give thanks for daily bread and especially for this communion bread. We remember Jesus and his great love for us. Thank you, God, for sending Jesus into the world and for the salvation he brings to each of us. Be present with us in spirit, O God, as we seek a renewal of mind and heart, so that our dedication may bear fruit in your name. Amen.

 In the quiet of these prayerful moments, O God, we pray for the ability to be more grateful for all you have done and continue to do for us. May Jesus and the meaning of this communion meal cause us to grasp more fully what happened in that upper room with the disciples. As we drink the cup, be receptive to our prayers. Urge us on in our daily quest for a meaningful and productive witness. Be close to us this coming week. Amen.

Redemptive God, who offers salvation to the world and to all your children of this earth, we thank you for the bread and food given to us this day. We break the bread of the Lord's Table in memory of Jesus, asking that your Spirit be within each one of us. We need you, O God, not only in moments of communion but also in our daily lives, as we dedicate ourselves to you. Amen.

Ever-giving God, we are grateful for your abundant gifts to us. As we drink this cup in the name of Jesus, may it be to us the cup of salvation. Be present in each one of us, O God, because without the guidance of your Holy Spirit, we cannot learn to follow in your pathway. Even in our rededication and commitment, we cannot go far without your guidance and continuing presence with us. Amen.

O Lord God, we give thanks that each day we receive food for the body. We pray that we may be more open to receive our needed bread of the Spirit. Bless the bread that we break here at the communion table. In this very act, O God, we remember Jesus and the assurance of eternal life. May your presence quicken our spirits so that your indwelling may be fruitful in our lives. Amen.

 Omnipotent God, in confidence and assurance we take this cup of blessing, knowing that you will not forsake us. In memory of Jesus we are present at this, his table. Make your presence known and felt within our hearts and minds so that our souls may be filled with your love. In dedication we look to the living of another week, and we ask your continued guidance as we seek to be your servants. Amen.

34

O God of mercy and forgiveness, help us to pause more often to give thanks for your provision of the bread we eat from day to day. May the breaking of the spiritual bread—as we commemorate once again the death, burial, and resurrection of Jesus—give sustenance to our lives. As we remember him, we ask your presence in each one of us, for we cannot walk life's path alone. We dedicate ourselves to walking more closely with you this coming week. Amen.

Loving God, we take the cup that reminds us of your promise for life eternal. Make us more mindful of that upper room as we remember Jesus' eating that Last Supper with his disciples. Be present with us as we drink the cup, realizing once again the price paid for our salvation. With a sense of assurance and renewal, we ask your continued presence to guide us in all that we do this coming week. Amen.

Lord of everything that we are, have been, and ever hope to be—we give thanks for your love, which provides our daily bread. An even greater evidence of your love is represented in the bread of this communion table. We thank you, O God, for Jesus and for his sacrificial love. May your Spirit dwell within us as we commit ourselves to serving your Kingdom. Amen.

 Spirit of the living God, descend upon our hearts and make us grateful as we take this cup of blessing in communion. Remembering Jesus makes us more aware of our shortcomings, but it encourages us to live boldly and confidently because he is our redeemer. We call upon you to be present in our drinking of the cup so that we might be renewed in commitment, following more closely in your way. Amen.

Eternal Creator, without your gift of bread we would die. Let us not starve our spirits but let us come with thanksgiving to eat of this communion bread today. Be present, O God, within us, so that even our prayers may be guided by your Spirit. Spur us on in our daily quest to be of greater service to you and to others. Amen.

Ever-present God, as we drink the cup, may it be a cup of thanksgiving for your love, which surrounds us and sustains us. By remembering Jesus, may our own confession of faith become a renewal of our commitment. Make us more effective instruments of your love, so that we might make this world a better place and may touch with good those persons who are around us. Amen.

Most caring God, we are grateful for your provision of food, clothing, and shelter. We break this bread of the Spirit, knowing we need both physical and spiritual sustenance in our lives. In memory of Jesus and in acknowledgment of his continued presence, we call upon you to fill us with renewed assurance of your love and care. We dedicate ourselves, O God, to your service. Amen.

 Eternal God, who loves us because of who we are more than for what we do, we give thanks as we take this cup. It is symbolic of Christ's sacrifice upon the cross. We remember him with gratitude and pray for the strengthening power of your Holy Spirit. Each one present prays for clearer understanding of your will for each of us. With a sense of renewal, we face more confidently the living of another week. Amen.

We thank you, O God, for not forsaking us when we turn to you in prayer. We thank you for daily bread and for the opportunity to partake of this bread of communion this morning. We remember Jesus and what his supper meant to those called so suddenly to continue his ministry. We need your presence if we are to continue in that ministry today. Bless our commitment to greater Christian service. Amen.

Eternal Creator, we seek your truth as we give thanks for this cup of communion, knowing how often we fall short of your will in our lives. In receiving the cup, we remember your Son, our Savior, and his redemptive power. Fill us with your Spirit, O God, so that with new awareness we may dedicate to you the days and weeks ahead. We ask your guidance in what we think, say, and do. Hear our prayer, O Lord. Amen.

O God, we come to you with uncertainty about the world around us, as well as with confusion about what is within us. In humility, we thank you for daily bread. We ask that you bless this bread that we break together at the Lord's Table. We honor and remember Jesus. Grant the indwelling of your Spirit as we rededicate ourselves to you. Amen.

 Bless, O God, to our comfort and strength this cup of communion. Thank you for the example that Jesus has set before us in service, life, and ministry. We pray for your presence within us, for without you our lives are empty and without direction. Guide us in our praying as well as in our living. O God, we commit our lives to you and ask your blessing. Amen.

Most patient God, in thanksgiving we seek your presence as we break bread together at this communion hour. We remember Jesus and his influence in our lives. We ask that your Holy Spirit may fill us and direct us. Grant, O God, that we may find renewal. Empower our commitment so that the days ahead may be lived in a way that is more pleasing in your sight. Amen.

Eternal God, thank you for creating us in your image. Empower us to live up to your expectations more completely. In giving thanks for the cup, we acknowledge your love in sending your Son, Jesus, who asks that we gather here and commune in his name. May we sense your presence, O God, so that there may be substance to our prayers of rededication this day. Amen.

41

Seeking your will for our lives, O God, we give thanks for daily bread and for the spiritual bread of this table. For the influence of Jesus across the ages in the lives of your people, we are most grateful. We call upon you to make known to us this day your will for our lives through your Holy Spirit. May the Lord's Supper bring us renewal today. Amen.

 O God, giver of every good and perfect gift, thank you for this cup. May it quench the thirst for your Spirit in each one of us. As we reflect on the meaning Jesus has brought into our lives, may we find renewed hope and strength that only you can give. In these high moments of rededication, bless each prayer that seeks guidance for living each day of this coming week. Amen.

Most caring God, we thank you in the name of your Son, Jesus, for the bread we break together at this communion hour. We remember that he not only instituted this Lord's Supper but also laid down his life for us on the cross so that we might know salvation. Receive, O God, our commitment for renewed effort to live for you during this coming week. Amen.

Almighty God, whose power we cannot comprehend, we give thanks for this cup and the meaning it represents as we drink it together each Sunday. May the message of the upper room, which Jesus gave to his disciples and to us, become more real, as each one here prays for self, for each other, and for the world. Amen.

For bringing us together around this table on the first day of another week, we give you thanks. We have received abundant daily bread to sustain our bodies. We come now to partake of the spiritual bread so that our spirits may be renewed. In memory of Jesus, and acknowledging his continuing presence, we break and eat this bread. May your Holy Spirit guide us in our renewal and our living in the days ahead. Amen.

 We are grateful, O God, for this cup and the life-giving blood of Jesus that it represents. Bless us as we drink the cup, and hear our prayers of rededication as we seek a closer walk with him who gave his life for us. May your presence, O God, be felt in our midst and within each seeking heart. We commit our lives to your keeping and our talents to your service. Be with us daily this coming week. Amen.

We realize, Loving God, that life is your greatest gift to us, and we give thanks for daily food. As we break and eat this communion bread, fill us anew with an awareness of your nearness and your presence with us. Instill within us your Spirit to help us live more worthily as you would have us live. Amen.

Infinite God, who knows no bounds of time or space, we take this cup in gratitude that you are our creator and ever-present God. In memory of Jesus, we drink together the cup of salvation, asking that your Spirit guide us in rededication. We are your children, seeking greater service in your Kingdom. Amen.

We give thanks for the loaf, O God, accepting it as the bread of life in these moments of communion. Fill us with your eternal Spirit, as we recall Jesus and his disciples in the upper room. Be present with us and active in guiding us as we rededicate ourselves to you this day. Amen.

 Merciful God, with thanksgiving we remember that we have been bought with so great a price. We drink together this wine in remembrance of Jesus, and we ask for your continued presence. We commit our lives to you—to serving you, and to serving others both near and far away. Use us daily for your purpose in life. Amen.

Caring God, we come together in thanksgiving for your blessing of daily bread, even as we break together the bread of the Spirit. Grant that our individual communion prayers may be acceptable in your sight. In memory of Jesus we come to this table. May your presence inspire us to renewed dedication to the task of Christian witness and service. Amen.

Eternal God, we are grateful for these common elements and the strength that enters our lives when we receive them as communion. Bless the cup we drink in memory of Jesus. May your presence remind us that with this privilege comes responsibility. Although we commit ourselves to more worthy service, we need your guidance for the living of each and every day. Amen.

We thank you for daily food, O God, remembering the hungry today and seeking ways in which they may be fed. In this memorial feast around the table, bless this spiritual bread, which we eat in memory of Jesus, our Lord. Be present in our lives as we renew our Christian intent and begin another week. Amen.

 God of life, accept our grateful thanks for this cup as we remember the sacrifice of Jesus on the cross. We are unworthy of that great love, yet in accepting him as our Savior we become his disciples. We call upon you to be present with us now as we make our commitment to living more intently as disciples of Christ in our day. Amen.

Eternal God, thank you for this bread of life, which binds us as one with Christians everywhere, as we gather around the table of the Lord. Forgive us for our shortsightedness and the many times we fall short of your will for our lives. Accept, O God, our prayers of penitence, petition, and gratitude in the silence of this hour. Guide us in the coming week as we seek to serve. Amen.

Most merciful God, we give our thanks for the privilege of seeing the dawn of another new day. As we receive the cup, may we be reminded of the price Jesus paid by giving his life upon the cross so that we might have assurance of eternal life. Be in our midst, O God, guiding not only our thoughts but our actions in the days that are to come. May our lives be lived for your glory. Amen.

In the breaking of bread around this communion table, we once again proclaim the good news of Jesus Christ. We accept him as the continuing Lord and Savior of our lives. Be near to us, O God, as we come to you individually in prayer. Go with each one of us as we return to our homes and prepare for living in a closer walk with you this coming week. Amen.

 As we hold in our hands and drink of this cup, we bring before you, O God, all that we have and are. Make of us more effective daily witnesses to the Kingdom you invite us to share in building, as evidence of our commitment and desire to serve you and those about us. Help us to live in such a way that others may know that we are your followers and workers in the unfinished task. Amen.

O God, we share with you in these
moments of Holy Communion, seeking
your comforting, sustaining, and guiding
presence. Thank you for daily bread and
for the spiritual bread of this communion table. We remember Jesus as we
bring to you our problems and disap-
pointments, our joy and anticipation of
days that lie ahead. Be with us as we
renew our commitment in breaking
bread. Amen.

Bless the cup, O God, and as we partake,
help us to recall in gratitude the upper
room where Jesus gave to his disciples,
and to all of us, the promise of salvation.
As we gather at the Lord's Table, may
your presence inspire us to deeper dedication because of all you have done for
us. Enrich our lives, and use them to
further your Kingdom here on earth, as
we seek to do our part in the week
ahead. Amen.

Almighty God, for your abiding presence and gift of daily bread, we give thanks. In the breaking of the spiritual bread in communion with you, we would remember Jesus and his redeeming love. Be present, O God, in our worship and time of rededication so that we may be strengthened and encouraged to live as you would have us to live in the days ahead. Amen.

 O God of time and eternity, we come in gratitude to this table of remembrance. As your gift of daily bread sustains our physical lives, may the cup and bread nourish us spiritually at this communion hour. In memory of Jesus, and because of what he means in our lives, we ask your presence and your blessing in our efforts to commit more fully our lives to you. Amen.

Gracious God, we give thanks for the opportunity of coming to this table to break bread. May the memory and the presence of Christ in our midst become more real to us. Grant that your Spirit may fill us so that our commitment may bear fruit in our daily lives in the week that lies before us. Enrich our joy in serving you and those about us. Amen.

In praise and thanksgiving we come to this table, O God, remembering as we receive the cup, our redemption through Jesus Christ. Hear our prayers as we ask that your presence be within each one of us this day. Help this moment of renewal and rededication to be fulfilled in our daily service to you and to those about us, as we seek to do our part in building your Kingdom. Amen.

O God, giver of life, we are grateful for bread, emerging as wheat from the soil and becoming the sustenance for our physical being. We praise you for the spiritual bread of the Lord's Table. We remember Jesus the night in which he was betrayed, and we pray that we might not betray his trust in us. Be present with us, O God, enabling us to fulfill our commitment and rededication. Amen.

 Everlasting God, whose love sustains us throughout our lives, we give thanks for this cup of the new covenant because of what Jesus has done for us. We remember how we received him as our Lord and Savior and accepted him as our guide for each day of our lives. We ask your presence now, as we drink the cup in a spirit of refreshed renewal, assured that you will not forsake us if we seek to do your will. Amen.

Merciful God, we thank you for our daily bread. We thank you for the bread of the spirit. We thank you for these moments of prayer and meditation. As we remember Jesus, may a renewed sense of his Spirit and your contributing presence become more alive and real in each one of us. We dedicate ourselves, O God, to renewal for the spiritual journey in the week that is to come. Amen.

We thank you for this cup, O God, asking that you make more real within us its meaning for our daily living. Guide our prayerful thoughts in remembering Jesus, his ministry, that upper room, his blessing of the bread and cup, his tragic death on the cross, and his triumph over death, which is our promise of life eternal. Be present with us, God, supporting and sustaining our commitment and rededication. Amen.

Eternal Spirit, in reverence we bring our prayers of thanksgiving for daily bread from the earth. May our thanks for your spiritual bread be even deeper as we come to this communion table. Enable the memory and presence of Jesus to instill in us the renewal that will empower us to greater service in the week to come. Amen.

 God of life, thank you for the cup. In the drinking of it we remember Jesus our Redeemer. Grant, O God, the deep indwelling of your Holy Spirit, in order that we may find joy, comfort, forgiveness, and encouragement for the life you would have us live. Without your presence and guidance, our prayers of rededication are empty and meaningless. Be with us in our daily living. Amen.

Infinite God, we give thanks for the mystery of life itself and for daily bread that nourishes our physical bodies. We pray that the spiritual bread may in like manner strengthen our souls. On the first day of another week, we recall Jesus and the upper room the night in which he was betrayed. Fill us with your Spirit now as we break together the bread of life. Strengthen our rededication, O God. Amen.

Ever-present God, with grateful hearts we take the cup with expectation and hope. As we remember Jesus, we do so as those who have accepted him as Lord and Savior. We call upon you, O God, to be present within and among us as we bring our individual prayers at this time of communion. We need the guidance of your Holy Spirit because we are so dependent upon you as our very source of life. Renew us, O God. Amen.

Immortal God, with thanksgiving for daily bread we come into your presence, grateful for this communion bread that revives our spirits. We acknowledge Jesus as Lord of our lives and remember him in grateful prayer. May your presence be with us in the breaking of bread. Help us, O God, to fulfill our vows of commitment as we commune together. Amen.

 God of love and life, we thank you that it is our privilege to gather here once again, as we have across the years, to praise your name and give thanks. This cup we drink, remembering not only the life and ministry of Jesus but also his promised presence as we come to his table. Grant us, O God, the renewal that comes to us and urges us to keep on trying to do your will through the days ahead. Amen.

God of all creation, and especially of
your children around the world, we give
thanks for daily bread, and we ask you
to guide us in feeding the hungry of this
earth. For this communion bread of the
Spirit, we are grateful. In the eating of it,
may we remember Jesus our Savior. We
rededicate ourselves, O God, to a life of
deepened spirit and daily witness this
coming week. Amen.

Omnipotent God, we are grateful that
we can depend upon your love and care,
even when we fall short of doing your
will in our daily lives. We thank you for
daily bread, which strengthens our
bodies, and now for this cup of the Spirit,
which recalls to us the presence of Christ
among us. In rededication we take the
bread and cup of communion, assured
of your presence to guide us this week.
Amen.

Everlasting God, whose love for us is without measure, we give thanks for the blessing of daily bread. May your gift of the Spirit through the breaking of communion bread enrich us spiritually as we come to this table. Bring to our minds the sacrifice of Jesus, as we ask for your presence within and among us, O God. Guide our thoughts and actions this coming week as we dedicate ourselves anew to the building of your Kingdom. Amen.

 God of the universe, may the power of your Spirit become an enabling power in our lives as we receive this cup of the Lord's Table. We remember Jesus on the night in which he was betrayed and ask that in what we think and do, we might not betray him in our own lives. Fill us with your Spirit, O God, that we might become more worthy instruments of your love and peace in our daily lives. Amen.

Gracious and sustaining God, forgive us for taking for granted the gift of daily bread. As we gather once again at this communion table, may the bread we eat here strengthen us spiritually for Christian living and witnessing in our world. We thank you for the gift of your Son, Jesus, as we pray silently in these moments of reflection and gratitude, O God. Fill us with a fresh awareness of your Holy Spirit in our lives. Use us in dedication as we are renewed for the living of another week. Amen.

Liberating God, we give thanks for the freedom with which we have been bought through Jesus Christ. May this cup we drink at this communion hour be truly a cup of blessing in our lives. We remember the sacrifice of your Son on the cross for our salvation. Unworthy as we are, O God, we call upon your guiding presence to be with us as we face and live the days that lie ahead. Amen.

God of love and beauty, thank you for the food that has sustained our bodies this past week. We break together this communion bread that we may be blessed spiritually as we have been blessed physically so that in renewed strength we might serve you and your Kingdom. We remember Jesus as we seek your divine presence to enable us to live more fully as you would have us live. Accept our thanks in the name of your Son. Amen.

 Eternal God, whose ever-present love illuminates our lives, we give thanks for the cup which we receive at this communion table. We remember Jesus taking the bread and breaking it and giving it to his disciples and are grateful that now we may enter into that same sense of belonging to the one who redeemed us. Be present in our midst as we dedicate ourselves this day so that as we leave this place of worship we are assured that we do not go out alone. Amen.

Almighty God, we stand in awe as we sense the miracles you have provided all around us. We are grateful for the provision of daily bread, which sustains our physical bodies. How much more we need the spiritual bread we receive at this table today. Help us, O God, to understand more completely your Son, Jesus, who died that we might live. Be present with us, O God, that our renewal and commitment might be filled with the power of your Spirit. Amen.

Steadfast God, you are the rock of ages and the anchor of our being. Without you, we are nothing, but with you we can be something. We drink this cup remembering Jesus and asking for a greater awareness of your presence as we come to the table of our Lord. Commit us, O God, to more worthy Christian love, sharing, and service in the opportunities that each day provides. Enable us, each day, to fulfill your mission for us in the world. Amen.

Ever-present God, thank you for daily bread that keeps alive the physical bodies you have given us. Help us not to neglect our spiritual needs, as we break together this bread, which recalls to us the sacrifice of Jesus upon the cross that we might be redeemed. Be present, O God, and help us to feel and know your power and your presence. Renew us and use us this coming week. Amen.

 Blessed God, we receive this cup of blessing remembering the price that was paid for our salvation. We give thanks for the willingness of Jesus to suffer, die, and become victorious that we might have eternal life. How grateful we are for the promise of the presence of your Holy Spirit within our lives, if we call upon you to be our ever-present counselor and guide. Accept, our God, the commitment that we bring in these moments of re-dedication at this table of our Savior. Bless our living in the days ahead. Amen.

Communion Prayers

Especially for

Advent Sunday
Christmas Sunday
New Year's Sunday
Palm Sunday
Maundy Thursday
Easter Sunday
Pentecost Sunday
Thanksgiving Sunday

Advent Sunday

 With this Advent season, O God, we pray for a renewed sense of its ageless meaning. Thank you for sending your Son into the world so that we may be saved. May we have a sense of awe and anticipation as we prepare ourselves for the coming of the Christ child. Bless this bread we break together here at the communion table. Be within us and use us as your children this Advent season. Amen.

 Ever-present God, fill us with the joy of the wise men and the shepherds of long ago as they awaited the coming of the Christ child. We receive this cup in prayer and thanksgiving at this time of rejoicing, because of our celebration of the event that is to come. In memory of Jesus we drink the cup, asking your abiding presence with us throughout this time of Advent. Bless our service. Amen.

Christmas Sunday

Eternal God, giver of life and immortality, thank you for the greatest gift of all time, the gift of Jesus your Son and our Savior, whose birth we celebrate this day. May the warmth and love of the Christmas season embrace our lives, especially in the breaking of bread on this day in which we commemorate the birth of Christ. Fill us with your Spirit so that we may share with others our Christmas joy. Amen.

O God, how grateful we are that the Word became flesh and dwelt among us! Thank you for sending your Son into the world as a babe lying in a manger. We join together at this communion meal at Christmas to celebrate his coming. May the cup we drink be a cup of blessing, as we seek a deeper sense of his presence, and may this Christmas be a time of renewed dedication to you. Amen.

New Year's Sunday

 God of history, who is always with us, we come into your presence at the beginning of another year to praise and to give thanks. May we in these moments of communion resolve to live, each day of the coming year, seeking to follow more closely in your way. We eat the bread, O God, in rededication and commitment to make this a new beginning. Amen.

 On this first Sunday of another new year, most loving God, we take this cup with a sense of newness and anticipation as we remember Jesus at his table. Grant us the insight, O God, to see more clearly the path you would have us follow in the days of the coming year. Be with us in our efforts to know your will and to serve you more faithfully. Amen.

Palm Sunday

On this Palm Sunday, O God, we hail
once again the triumphal entry of Jesus
into the ancient city of Jerusalem. In our
breaking of the bread, we commemorate
the joy and seeming triumph, which only
a few days later ended in despair. We
pray for steadfastness, that we may not
lose hope in our time of fear. May your
Holy Spirit guide us throughout this
week. Amen.

God of us, all, at the beginning of another
observance of the Easter Week, we are
reminded how easy it is to lose our faith,
even as did the people of long ago after
their Hosannas of Palm Sunday. Bless
this cup of renewal, and fill us with your
Spirit. May this Holy Week be for us
truly a holy one. Guide and direct us in
the living of it. Amen.

Maundy Thursday

 We come together this Maundy Thursday evening to commemorate in a service of communion the last supper of Jesus with his disciples, O God. As we eat the bread, may we sense what the disciples felt as they were told that the next day Jesus would be tried, condemned, and crucified on a cross. Most loving God, be close to us as you were to them, and bless us now. Amen.

 Compassionate God, whose love for us was so great that you gave your Son so that we might receive salvation, bless this cup, even as Jesus blessed the cup in the upper room. Like his disciples, we do not understand, but Jesus reminds us that as often as we eat the bread and drink the cup of his table, we do so in memory of him. Be present with us in the quiet of this Maundy Thursday service of communion. Amen.

Easter Sunday

Redemptive God, we give thanks this day for the triumph and victory of Easter, with its promise of life eternal. With grateful hearts we receive the bread, recalling to our minds the suffering of Jesus and his death upon the cross. The triumph of Easter morning demonstrates that hope was not in vain. Hope became a reality and assures of the continuing presence of Christ in our lives. Bless us now, we pray. Amen.

Oh God, whose love was so great that you sent your Son into the world to die for our sins, our thanksgiving is more vivid on Easter. As we celebrate the fulfilling of the prophecy of Jesus that he would not forsake his disciples, we acknowledge his salvation promised to each one of us. In drinking of this cup, we remember how priceless is the Lord's Table. Be present with us, and may your Spirit enrich us in the days ahead. Amen.

Pentecost Sunday

 At Pentecost, O God, we give thanks for the church and its survival through the centuries. With so great a cloud of witnesses, we are given heart as we break and eat in rededication this element of our salvation. May we experience individually the blessing of the Holy Spirit, that we might live Spirit-filled lives in the week to come. Amen.

 Caring God, enable us to be worthy members of your church as we celebrate its beginnings. Thank you for its continuing influence in human life when we open ourselves to the indwelling of your Spirit. Bless, O God, this cup of remembrance, and may a spirit such as that at Pentecost pervade our lives this day as we drink the cup of this communion table. Guide us in daily living. Amen.

Thanksgiving Sunday

We should always be grateful, O God, but especially at Thanksgiving we are reminded of your bounty. For the bread that nourishes our inner need, we give thanks as we eat here at the Lord's Table. May the harvest of our lives be evident as we seek your indwelling Spirit, which helps us live our days in usefulness. Amen.

Spirit of the living God, enter into our lives with renewed meaning at this season of Thanksgiving. May we always give thanks for the yield of the soil, which provides our daily food. May this cup remind us again of Jesus and his presence, even as we ask for a continued walk with you in our journey of life. Use us to extend your Kingdom. Amen.

Communion Record Pages

The following pages are provided for use if they prove to be helpful.

In some congregations, this book is passed on to the elder serving at the communion table on the next Sunday.

There is value in noting which prayers have been used by glancing at the following pages. These pages should be filled in from Sunday to Sunday.

If this is your own copy of the book, you may still wish to check and date the Communion Record Pages.

Communion Record			
	Please check:		Write in Date
Page #	Bread	Cup	
9			
10			
11			
12			
13			
14			
15			
16			
17			
18			
19			
20			
21			
22			
23			
24			
25			
26			

Communion Record			
Page #	Please check:		Write in Date
	Bread	Cup	
27			
28			
29			
30			
31			
32			
33			
34			
35			
36			
37			
38			
39			
40			
41			
42			
43			
44			

Communion Record			
	Please check:		Write in Date
Page #	Bread	Cup	
45			
46			
47			
48			
49			
50			
51			
52			
53			
54			
55			
56			
57			
58			
59			
60			
61			
62			

Communion Record			
	Please check:		Write in Date
Page #	Bread	Cup	
63			
66			
67			
68			
69			
70			
71			
72			
73			

A Closing Word

If this book has been helpful to you as an elder, suggest that other elders in your congregation secure a copy.

If the intent of this book has been fulfilled, your thoughts should flow more freely in the preparation and writing of your own communion prayers.

This is the goal.

God bless you in your efforts toward achieving this goal. Reread the introduction and the Elder's Prayer occasionally as you pursue your task.

Shalom, R. F. H.